The MAILBOX®
The Education Center®

grade 1

Phenomenal Phonics®

Phonics Games

Reproducible Lotto Games for Reinforcing

W9-AZR-933

- ## Word Families

- ## Vowels

- ## Blends

Managing Editor: Gerri Primak

Editorial Team: Becky S. Andrews, Kimberley Bruck, Karen P. Shelton, Diane Badden, Thad H. McLaurin, Sharon Murphy, Lynn Drolet, Kelly Robertson, Karen A. Brudnak, Juli Docimo Blair, Hope Rodgers, Dorothy C. McKinney

Production Team: Lori Z. Henry, Pam Crane, Rebecca Saunders, Jennifer Tipton Cappoen, Chris Curry, Sarah Foreman, Theresa Lewis Goode, Greg D. Rieves, Eliseo De Jesus Santos II, Barry Slate, Donna K. Teal, Zane Williard, Tazmen Carlisle, Kathy Coop, Marsha Heim, Lynette Dickerson, Mark Rainey, Amy Kirtley-Hill

Reproducible Assessments Also Included!

www.themailbox.com

©2007 The Mailbox®
All rights reserved.
ISBN10 #1-56234-748-9 • ISBN13 #978-156234-748-2

Manufactured in the United States
10 9 8 7 6 5 4 3 2 1

Table of Contents

Lotto Games

Assessments

What's Inside

Phonics Games contains ten reproducible lotto games, each reinforcing a different skill. Each game includes the following:

- directions for the teacher
- six different reproducible gameboards
- reproducible teacher cards
- a reproducible follow-up assessment page

Teacher Directions

Gameboards

Teacher Cards

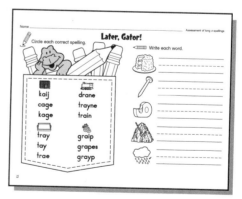

Assessment Page

Also Included:
- assessment pages to review word families, vowels, and blends
- reproducible student brag tags
- reproducible storage labels

Brag Tags

Copy onto colorful construction paper, cut out, and use as rewards for each game.

You're Sharp!

TEC61062

What a Treat!

TEC61062

_____ is a busy beaver!

TEC61062

Way to go!

TEC61062

_____ is
name

shining bright with phonics!

_____
teacher

_____
date

Off to School
Short a Word Families Game

What you need:

- gameboard copy (pages 7–9) for each player

- game markers, such as ¾" construction paper squares

- copy of the reproducible teacher cards (pages 10 and 11), cut apart, shuffled, and placed in an envelope

Dinosaurs on Board

Directions:

1. Give game markers and a gameboard to each child. Have him read each word family heading and then read the words in the corresponding columns. Provide assistance as necessary.

2. Explain that when he hears a word, he identifies the word family and then reads the words in that column. If the word is written on his board, he is to cover it with a marker.

3. Describe the criteria for winning: three in a row (vertically, horizontally, or diagonally), four corners, or fill the board. Ask that winners say, "Beep, beep!" to signal their wins.

4. To play, remove a card from the envelope and read it aloud. (Place it faceup for your later reference.) Students who have the matching word cover it.

5. Play continues until someone calls out, "Beep, beep!" To verify his win, have him uncover and read each word as you check his responses.

DiNo Bus

See page 66 for a student assessment page.

Off to School
Short a Word Families Game

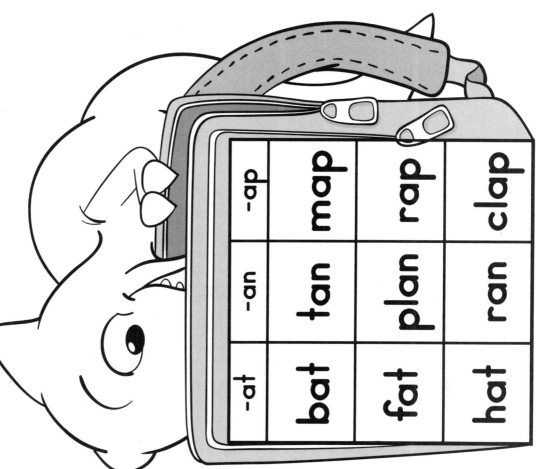

-ap	-an	-at
map	tan	bat
rap	plan	fat
clap	ran	hat

Off to School
Short a Word Families Game

-ap	-an	-at
lap	fan	pat
trap	van	rat
nap	man	cat

7

Off to School
Short a Word Families Game

-at	-an	-ap
sat	pan	slap
cat	tan	rap
mat	can	flap

Off to School
Short a Word Families Game

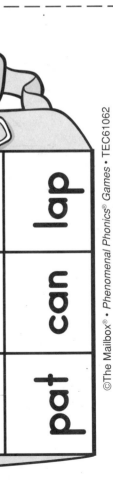

-at	-an	-ap
fat	ran	sap
chat	man	tap
pat	can	lap

Off to School
Short a Word Families Game

-at	-an	-ap
hat	than	cap
mat	fan	snap
rat	pan	map

Off to School
Short a Word Families Game

-at	-an	-ap
pat	van	flap
that	can	nap
bat	plan	sap

bat TEC61062	**cat** TEC61062	**chat** TEC61062
fat TEC61062	**hat** TEC61062	**mat** TEC61062
pat TEC61062	**rat** TEC61062	**sat** TEC61062
that TEC61062	**can** TEC61062	**fan** TEC61062
man TEC61062	**pan** TEC61062	**plan** TEC61062
ran TEC61062	**tan** TEC61062	**than** TEC61062

van TEC61062	cap TEC61062	clap TEC61062
flap TEC61062	lap TEC61062	map TEC61062
nap TEC61062	rap TEC61062	sap TEC61062
slap TEC61062	snap TEC61062	tap TEC61062
trap TEC61062		

Sunken Treasure
Short i Word Families Game

What you need:
- gameboard copy (pages 13–15) for each player
- game markers, such as ¾" construction paper squares
- copy of the reproducible teacher cards (pages 16 and 17), cut apart, shuffled, and placed in an envelope

Directions:

1. Give game markers and a gameboard to each child. Have her read each word family heading and then read the words in the corresponding columns. Provide assistance as necessary.

2. Explain that when she hears a word, she identifies the word family and then reads the words in that column. If the word is written on her board, she is to cover it with a marker.

3. Describe the criteria for winning: three in a row (vertically, horizontally, or diagonally), four corners, or fill the board. Ask that winners say, "Sunken treasure!" to signal their wins.

4. To play, remove a card from the envelope and read it aloud. (Place it faceup for your later reference.) Students who have the matching word cover it.

5. Play continues until someone calls out, "Sunken treasure!" To verify her win, have her uncover and read each word as you check her responses.

See page 67 for a student assessment page.

Sunken Treasure
Short *i* Word Families Game

-in	-ip	-ick
win	hip	click
grin	lip	pick
bin	sip	thick

Sunken Treasure
Short *i* Word Families Game

-in	-ip	-ick
pin	dip	lick
fin	rip	brick
spin	chip	kick

Sunken Treasure
Short *i* Word Families Game

-in	-ip	-ick
tin	clip	pick
bin	whip	kick
fin	lip	stick

Sunken Treasure
Short *i* Word Families Game

-in	-ip	-ick
skin	tip	quick
pin	dip	pick
thin	ship	sick

Sunken Treasure
Short *i* Word Families Game

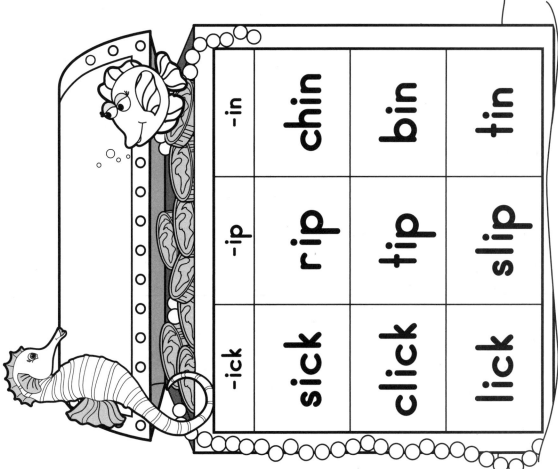

-in	-ip	-ick
chin	rip	sick
bin	tip	click
tin	slip	lick

Sunken Treasure
Short *i* Word Families Game

-in	-ip	-ick
win	flip	kick
chin	hip	lick
fin	sip	chick

Reproducible Teacher Cards
Use with the directions on page 12.

brick TEC61062	chick TEC61062	click TEC61062
kick TEC61062	lick TEC61062	pick TEC61062
quick TEC61062	sick TEC61062	stick TEC61062
thick TEC61062	chip TEC61062	clip TEC61062
dip TEC61062	flip TEC61062	hip TEC61062
lip TEC61062	rip TEC61062	ship TEC61062

sip TEC61062	slip TEC61062	tip TEC61062
whip TEC61062	bin TEC61062	chin TEC61062
fin TEC61062	grin TEC61062	pin TEC61062
skin TEC61062	spin TEC61062	thin TEC61062
tin TEC61062	win TEC61062	

Soup's On!
Short o Word Families Game

What you need:

- gameboard copy (pages 19–21) for each player

- game markers, such as ¾" construction paper squares

- copy of the reproducible teacher cards (pages 22 and 23), cut apart, shuffled, and placed in an envelope

Directions:

1. Give game markers and a gameboard to each child. Have him read each word family heading and then read the words in the corresponding columns. Provide assistance as necessary.

2. Explain that when he hears a word, he identifies the word family and then reads the words in that column. If the word is written on his board, he is to cover it with a marker.

3. Describe the criteria for winning: three in a row (vertically, horizontally, or diagonally), four corners, or fill the board. Ask that winners say, "Soup's on!" to signal their wins.

4. To play, remove a card from the envelope and read it aloud. (Place it faceup for your later reference.) Students who have the matching word cover it.

5. Play continues until someone calls out, "Soup's on!" To verify his win, have him uncover and read each word as you check his responses.

See page 68 for a student assessment page.

Soup's On!
Short o Word Families Game

-ot	-op	-ock
cot	mop	flock
hot	top	sock
pot	shop	dock

Soup's On!
Short o Word Families Game

-ot	-op	-ock
got	prop	stock
dot	hop	rock
trot	cop	block

19

Soup's On!
Short *o* Word Families Game

-ot	-op	-ock
dot	flop	rock
rot	pop	smock
hot	crop	lock

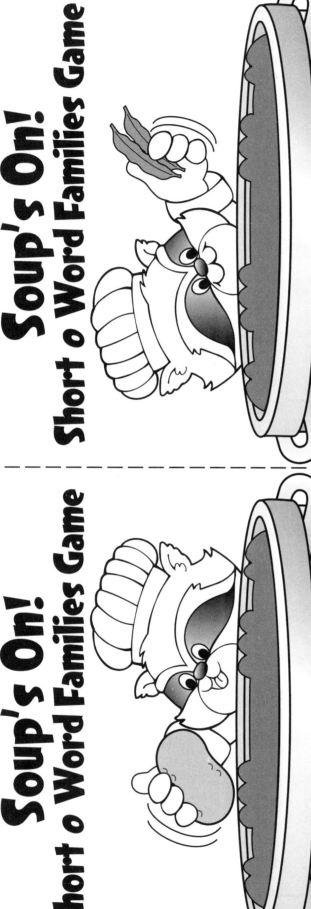

Soup's On!
Short *o* Word Families Game

-ot	-op	-ock
lot	bop	clock
slot	stop	dock
tot	mop	sock

Soup's On!
Short o Word Families Game

-ock	-op	-ot
sock	slop	pot
dock	hop	blot
lock	plop	not

Soup's On!
Short o Word Families Game

-ock	-op	-ot
shock	top	cot
rock	cop	got
lock	hop	spot

block TEC61062	clock TEC61062	dock TEC61062
flock TEC61062	lock TEC61062	rock TEC61062
shock TEC61062	smock TEC61062	sock TEC61062
stock TEC61062	bop TEC61062	cop TEC61062
crop TEC61062	flop TEC61062	hop TEC61062
mop TEC61062	plop TEC61062	pop TEC61062

prop TEC61062	shop TEC61062	slop TEC61062
stop TEC61062	top TEC61062	blot TEC61062
cot TEC61062	dot TEC61062	got TEC61062
hot TEC61062	lot TEC61062	not TEC61062
pot TEC61062	rot TEC61062	slot TEC61062
spot TEC61062	tot TEC61062	trot TEC61062

Yummy Honey!
Short u Word Families Game

What you need:

- gameboard copy (pages 25–27) for each player
- game markers, such as ¾" construction paper squares
- copy of the reproducible teacher cards (pages 28 and 29), cut apart, shuffled, and placed in an envelope

Directions:

1. Give game markers and a gameboard to each child. Have her read each word family heading and then read the words in the corresponding columns. Provide assistance as necessary.

2. Explain that when she hears a word, she identifies the word family and then reads the words in that column. If the word is written on her board, she is to cover it with a marker.

3. Describe the criteria for winning: three in a row (vertically, horizontally, or diagonally), four corners, or fill the board. Ask that winners say, "Yummy honey!" to signal their wins.

4. To play, remove a card from the envelope and read it aloud. (Place it faceup for your later reference.) Students who have the matching word cover it.

5. Play continues until someone calls out, "Yummy honey!" To verify her win, have her uncover and read each word as you check her responses.

See page 69 for a student assessment page.

Yummy Honey!
Short *u* Word Families Game

-uck	-ug	-ump
puck	mug	thump
cluck	rug	bump
tuck	chug	jump

Yummy Honey!
Short *u* Word Families Game

-uck	-ug	-ump
luck	bug	plump
puck	tug	hump
duck	snug	stump

Yummy Honey!
Short u Word Families Game

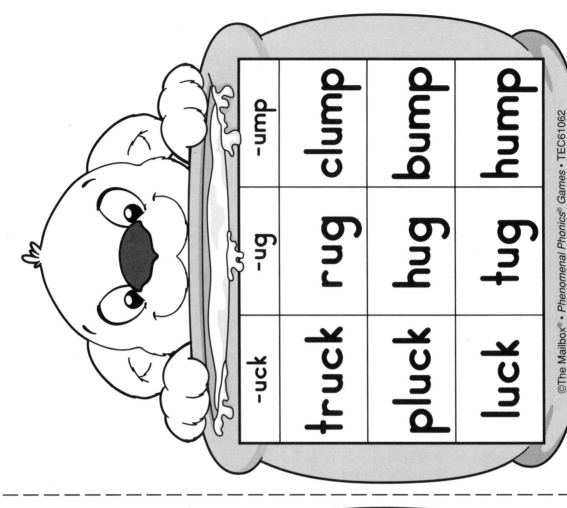

-uck	-ug	-ump
truck	rug	clump
pluck	hug	bump
luck	tug	hump

Yummy Honey!
Short u Word Families Game

-uck	-ug	-ump
duck	plug	lump
stuck	jug	dump
yuck	dug	pump

Yummy Honey!
Short *u* Word Families Game

-uck	-ug	-ump
luck	dug	pump
duck	plug	thump
stuck	mug	lump

Yummy Honey!
Short *u* Word Families Game

-uck	-ug	-ump
snuck	hug	dump
tuck	bug	jump
puck	jug	stump

cluck TEC61062	duck TEC61062	luck TEC61062
pluck TEC61062	puck TEC61062	snuck TEC61062
stuck TEC61062	truck TEC61062	tuck TEC61062
yuck TEC61062	bug TEC61062	chug TEC61062
dug TEC61062	hug TEC61062	jug TEC61062

mug TEC61062	plug TEC61062	rug TEC61062
snug TEC61062	tug TEC61062	bump TEC61062
clump TEC61062	dump TEC61062	hump TEC61062
jump TEC61062	lump TEC61062	plump TEC61062
pump TEC61062	stump TEC61062	thump TEC61062

Special Delivery
Blends Game

sk, sl, sn, sp, st, sw

What you need:
- gameboard copy (pages 31–33) for each player
- game markers, such as ¾" construction paper squares
- copy of the reproducible teacher cards (pages 34 and 35), cut apart, shuffled, and placed in an envelope

Directions:

1. Give game markers and a gameboard to each child. Review the blend sounds featured on each gameboard.

2. Explain that when she hears a word, she listens for its beginning blend. If the matching blend is on her board, she is to cover it with a marker.

3. Describe the criteria for winning: four in a row (horizontally, vertically, or diagonally) or four corners. Ask that winners say, "Special delivery!" to signal their wins.

4. To play, remove a card from the envelope and say the name of the picture aloud. If desired, also show students the picture card. (Place it faceup for your later reference.) Students who have a matching blend cover it. (A child may cover only one blend at a time.)

5. Play continues until someone calls out, "Special delivery!" To verify her win, have her uncover and say the sound of each blend as you check her responses.

See page 71 for a student assessment page.

Special Delivery Blends Game

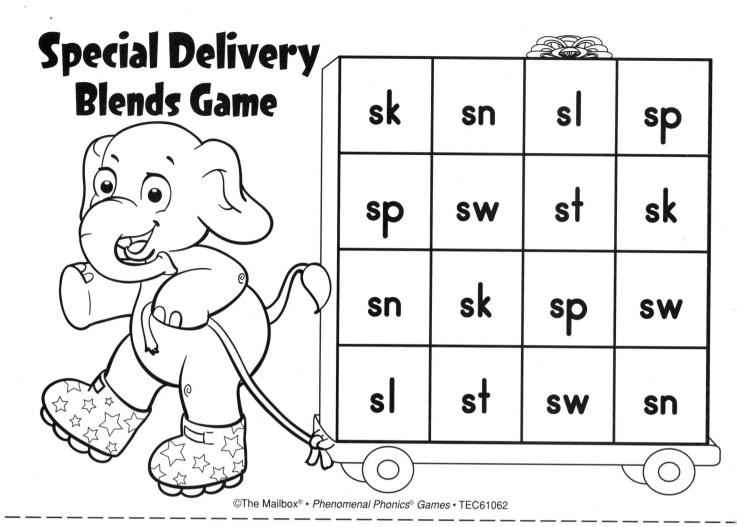

sk	sn	sl	sp
sp	sw	st	sk
sn	sk	sp	sw
sl	st	sw	sn

Special Delivery Blends Game

sl	sw	sp	sn
st	sp	sk	sl
sn	st	sw	sk
sw	sl	sn	st

Special Delivery
Blends Game

sn	sw	st	sk
sw	sl	sn	sp
sl	sp	sk	sn
st	sk	sl	sw

Special Delivery
Blends Game

sp	sk	sl	sw
sn	sw	st	sp
st	sl	sn	sk
sk	st	sp	sl

Special Delivery Blends Game

st	sw	sp	sl
sw	sl	st	sn
sk	sn	sw	sp
sp	st	sn	sk

Special Delivery Blends Game

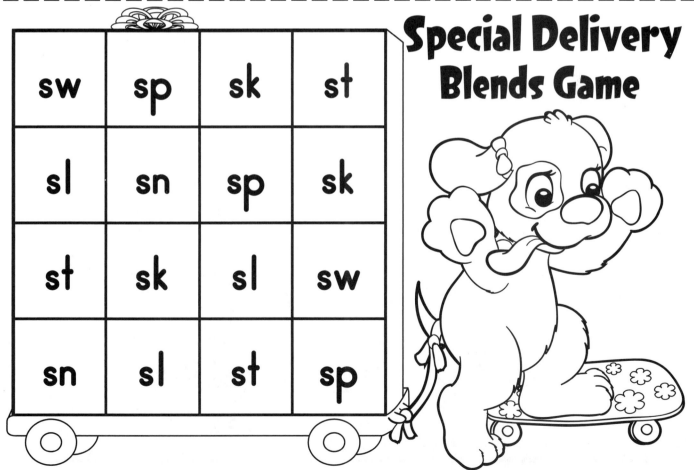

sw	sp	sk	st
sl	sn	sp	sk
st	sk	sl	sw
sn	sl	st	sp

Reproducible Teacher Cards

Use with the directions on page 30.

TEC61062

TEC61062

TEC61062

TEC61062

TEC61062

TEC61062

TEC61062

TEC61062

TEC61062

TEC61062

TEC61062

TEC61062

TEC61062

TEC61062

TEC61062

TEC61062

TEC61062

TEC61062

Hanging Out to Dry

Blends Game

bl, br, cl, cr, fl, fr, gl, gr

What you need:

- gameboard copy (pages 37–39) for each player
- game markers, such as ¾" construction paper squares
- copy of the reproducible teacher cards (pages 40 and 41), cut apart, shuffled, and placed in an envelope

Directions:

1. Give game markers and a gameboard to each child. Review the blend sounds featured on each gameboard.

2. Explain that when he hears a word, he listens for its beginning blend. If the matching blend is on his board, he is to cover it with a marker.

3. Describe the criteria for winning: four in a row (horizontally, vertically, or diagonally) or four corners. Ask that winners say, "Tweet, tweet!" to signal their wins.

4. To play, remove a card from the envelope and say the name of the picture aloud. If desired, also show students the picture card. (Place it faceup for your later reference.) Students who have a matching blend cover it. (A child may cover only one blend at a time.)

5. Play continues until someone calls out, "Tweet, tweet!" To verify his win, have him uncover and say the sound of each blend as you check his responses.

See page 72 for a student assessment page.

Hanging Out to Dry
Blends Game

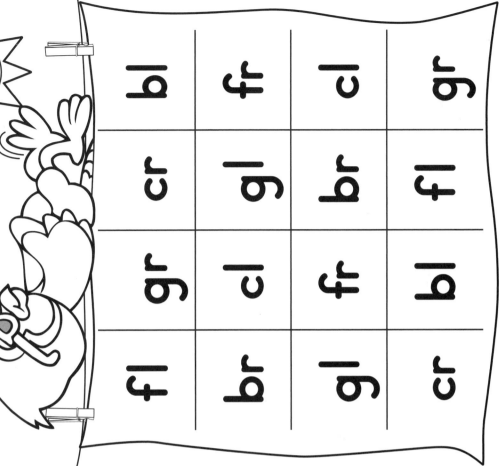

bl	cr	gr	fl
ff	gl	cl	br
cl	br	fr	gl
gr	fl	bl	cr

Hanging Out to Dry
Blends Game

cl	gl	fr	bl
gr	cr	gl	cl
bl	fr	fl	br
br	fl	cr	gr

Hanging Out to Dry
Blends Game

cr	bl	ff
gr	fl	gl
cl	br	cl
bl	cr	ff

gl	br	fl	gl

Hanging Out to Dry
Blends Game

cl	br	cl
fl	gr	fl
gr	cr	gr
br	cl	br

gl	ff	cr	ff

Hanging Out to Dry
Blends Game

fl	bl	fr	gr
br	cr	bl	gl
gr	br	gl	cl
cl	fl	cr	fr

Hanging Out to Dry
Blends Game

cr	bl	fr	br
br	fr	cl	fl
gl	gr	bl	cr
fl	cl	gr	gl

Reproducible Teacher Cards

Use with the directions on page 36.

TEC61062

TEC61062

TEC61062

TEC61062

TEC61062

TEC61062

TEC61062

TEC61062

TEC61062

TEC61062

TEC61062

TEC61062

TEC61062

TEC61062

TEC61062

TEC61062

Later, Gator!
Long a Game

What you need:

- gameboard copy (pages 43–45) for each player

- game markers, such as ¾" construction paper squares

- copy of the reproducible teacher cards (pages 46 and 47), cut apart, shuffled, and placed in an envelope

Directions:

1. Give game markers and a gameboard to each child. Have her read each word on her board, noting the different spellings of long *a*. Provide assistance as necessary.

2. Explain that when she hears a word that is written on her board, she is to cover it with a marker.

3. Describe the criteria for winning: four in a row (vertically, horizontally, or diagonally) or four corners. Ask that winners say, "Later, gator!" to signal their wins.

4. To play, remove a card from the envelope and read it aloud. (Place it faceup in alphabetical order for your later reference.) Students who have the matching word cover it.

5. Play continues until someone calls out, "Later, gator!" To verify her win, have her uncover and read each word as you check her responses.

See page 73 for a student assessment page.

Later, Gator!
Long a Game

bait	cave	say	maid
cape	grain	brain	cage
way	may	place	mail
nail	flake	fail	late

Later, Gator!
Long a Game

day	came	pail	late
way	paint	tray	frame
cake	gray	grape	pain
hay	paid	lane	aim

Later, Gator!
Long *a* Game

paid	face	stay	mail
rail	gray	whale	make
day	pain	date	race
train	take	say	grape

Later, Gator!
Long *a* Game

SEEDS

bake	faint	sale	main
rain	made	race	wait
pail	braid	gate	clay
play	chase	tray	jay

Later, Gator!
Long a Game

bake	whale	jay	tail
made	faint	came	wait
tape	chase	fail	place
flake	rail	sale	brain

Later, Gator!
Long a Game

lake	main	bait	ate
tray	same	clay	braid
base	play	tame	maid
grain	date	way	tape

aim	bait	braid	brain	fail
faint	grain	maid	mail	main
nail	paid	pail	pain	paint
rail	rain	tail	train	wait
clay	day	gray	hay	jay
may	play	say	stay	

Each card is labeled: TEC61062

tray	way	ate	bake	base
TEC61062	TEC61062	TEC61062	TEC61062	TEC61062
cage	cake	came	cape	cave
TEC61062	TEC61062	TEC61062	TEC61062	TEC61062
chase	date	face	flake	frame
TEC61062	TEC61062	TEC61062	TEC61062	TEC61062
gate	grape	lake	lane	late
TEC61062	TEC61062	TEC61062	TEC61062	TEC61062
made	make	place	race	sale
TEC61062	TEC61062	TEC61062	TEC61062	TEC61062
same	take	tame	tape	whale
TEC61062	TEC61062	TEC61062	TEC61062	TEC61062

Time for Ice Cream
Long *i* Game

What you need:
- gameboard copy (pages 49–51) for each player
- game markers, such as ¾" construction paper squares
- copy of the reproducible teacher cards (pages 52 and 53), cut apart, shuffled, and placed in an envelope

Directions:

1. Give game markers and a gameboard to each child. Have him read each word on his board, noting the different spellings of long *i*. Provide assistance as necessary.

2. Explain that when he hears a word that is written on his board, he is to cover it with a marker.

3. Describe the criteria for winning: four in a row (vertically, horizontally, or diagonally) or four corners. Ask that winners say, "Yum, yum!" to signal their wins.

4. To play, remove a card from the envelope and read it aloud. (Place it faceup in alphabetical order for your later reference.) Students who have the matching word cover it.

5. Play continues until someone calls out, "Yum, yum!" To verify his win, have him uncover and read each word as you check his responses.

See page 74 for a student assessment page.

Time for Ice Cream
Long *i* Game

right	spike	pie	my
prize	time	fly	kite
lie	pine	high	night
fight	shy	dive	shine

Time for Ice Cream
Long *i* Game

bite	life	tie	flight
ripe	cry	five	wide
try	tight	pie	slide
hide	pine	bike	pry

Time for Ice Cream
Long *i* Game

light	white	sky	fright
slice	pie	lie	line
mine	by	sigh	rise
die	bike	like	fry

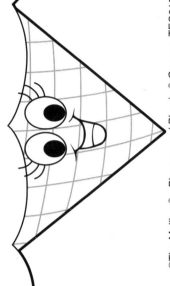

Time for Ice Cream
Long *i* Game

dry	tie	fry	dime
pipe	ice	bright	thigh
might	why	price	spy
die	slide	fight	line

Time for Ice Cream
Long *i* Game

bright	sly	spike	my
slide	tie	wide	try
like	why	light	time
pie	might	dry	kite

Time for Ice Cream
Long *i* Game

sky	right	fly	pry
high	lie	nine	sight
wise	sight	by	hide
cry	flight	life	die

die TEC61062	**lie** TEC61062	**pie** TEC61062	**tie** TEC61062	**bike** TEC61062
bite TEC61062	**dime** TEC61062	**dive** TEC61062	**five** TEC61062	**hide** TEC61062
ice TEC61062	**kite** TEC61062	**life** TEC61062	**like** TEC61062	**line** TEC61062
mine TEC61062	**nine** TEC61062	**pine** TEC61062	**pipe** TEC61062	**price** TEC61062
prize TEC61062	**ripe** TEC61062	**rise** TEC61062	**shine** TEC61062	**slice** TEC61062
slide TEC61062	**spike** TEC61062	**time** TEC61062	**white** TEC61062	**wide** TEC61062

wise	high	sigh		
TEC61062	TEC61062	TEC61062		
thigh	bright	fight	flight	fright
TEC61062	TEC61062	TEC61062	TEC61062	TEC61062
light	might	night	right	sight
TEC61062	TEC61062	TEC61062	TEC61062	TEC61062
slight	tight	by	cry	dry
TEC61062	TEC61062	TEC61062	TEC61062	TEC61062
fly	fry	my	pry	shy
TEC61062	TEC61062	TEC61062	TEC61062	TEC61062
sky	sly	spy	try	why
TEC61062	TEC61062	TEC61062	TEC61062	TEC61062

Eager Beaver Long e Game

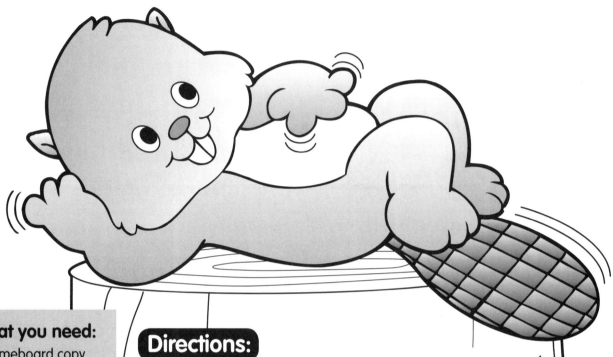

What you need:

- gameboard copy (pages 55–57) for each player

- game markers, such as ¾" construction paper squares

- copy of the reproducible teacher cards (pages 58 and 59), cut apart, shuffled, and placed in an envelope

Directions:

1. Give game markers and a gameboard to each child. Have her read each word on her board, noting the different spellings of long *e*. Provide assistance as necessary.

2. Explain that when she hears a word that is written on her board, she is to cover it with a marker.

3. Describe the criteria for winning: four in a row (vertically, horizontally, or diagonally) or four corners. Ask that winners say, "Eager beaver!" to signal their wins.

4. To play, remove a card from the envelope and read it aloud. (Place it faceup for your later reference.) Students who have the matching word cover it.

5. Play continues until someone calls out, "Eager beaver!" To verify her win, have her uncover and read each word as you check her responses.

See page 75 for a student assessment page.

Eager Beaver
Long e Game

beak	theme	dream	eve
peach	deep	green	neat
lean	bean	seem	cheese
peel	meet	heat	tea

Eager Beaver
Long e Game

bead	cheek	meal	teeth
seek	pea	read	clean
eat	beef	weed	free
seal	these	beat	team

Eager Beaver
Long e Game

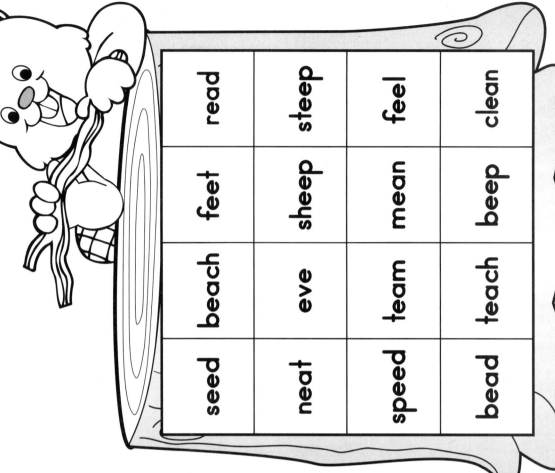

read	feet	beach	seed
steep	sheep	eve	neat
feel	mean	team	speed
clean	beep	teach	bead

Eager Beaver
Long e Game

treat	leave	beam	reach
flea	steep	greet	each
need	feed	peak	these
seen	seat	tree	bee

Eager Beaver
Long e Game

beam	sleep	tea	beat
flea	feed	theme	peel
seat	beef	cheese	reach
these	heat	weed	seek

Eager Beaver
Long e Game

east	mean	steep	fee
seal	pea	eve	feel
theme	meet	sheet	tree
deep	cheek	eat	beak

Reproducible Teacher Cards

Use with the directions on page 54.

beach TEC61062	**bead** TEC61062	**beak** TEC61062	**beam** TEC61062	**bean** TEC61062
beat TEC61062	**clean** TEC61062	**dream** TEC61062	**each** TEC61062	**east** TEC61062
eat TEC61062	**flea** TEC61062	**heat** TEC61062	**lean** TEC61062	**leave** TEC61062
meal TEC61062	**mean** TEC61062	**neat** TEC61062	**pea** TEC61062	**peach** TEC61062
peak TEC61062	**reach** TEC61062	**read** TEC61062	**seal** TEC61062	**seat** TEC61062
tea TEC61062	**teach** TEC61062	**team** TEC61062	**treat** TEC61062	**bee** TEC61062

©The Mailbox® • *Phenomenal Phonics*® *Games* • TEC61062

beef	beep	cheek	cheese	deep
TEC61062	TEC61062	TEC61062	TEC61062	TEC61062
fee	feed	feel	feet	free
TEC61062	TEC61062	TEC61062	TEC61062	TEC61062
green	greet	meet	need	peel
TEC61062	TEC61062	TEC61062	TEC61062	TEC61062
seed	seek	seem	seen	sheep
TEC61062	TEC61062	TEC61062	TEC61062	TEC61062
sheet	sleep	speed	steep	teeth
TEC61062	TEC61062	TEC61062	TEC61062	TEC61062
tree	weed	eve	theme	these
TEC61062	TEC61062	TEC61062	TEC61062	TEC61062

Mole's Garden
Long o Game

What you need:

- gameboard copy (pages 61–63) for each player

- game markers, such as ¾" construction paper squares

- copy of the reproducible teacher cards (pages 64 and 65), cut apart, shuffled, and placed in an envelope

Directions:

1. Give game markers and a gameboard to each child. Have him read each word on his board, noting the different spellings of long o. Provide assistance as necessary.

2. Explain that when he hears a word that is written on his board, he is to cover it with a marker.

3. Describe the criteria for winning: four in a row (vertically, horizontally, or diagonally) or four corners. Ask that winners say, "Mole's garden!" to signal their wins.

4. To play, remove a card from the envelope and read it aloud. (Place it faceup in alphabetical order for your later reference.) Students who have the matching word cover it.

5. Play continues until someone calls out, "Mole's garden!" To verify his win, have him uncover and read each word as you check his responses.

See page 76 for a student assessment page.

Mole's Garden
Long o Game

hope	note	mow	road
soap	doe	rose	robe
tone	stone	broke	snow
loan	glow	code	goat

Mole's Garden
Long o Game

toe	zone	goal	bone
hole	vote	foe	boat
smoke	show	roast	those
float	joke	low	rope

Mole's Garden
Long o Game

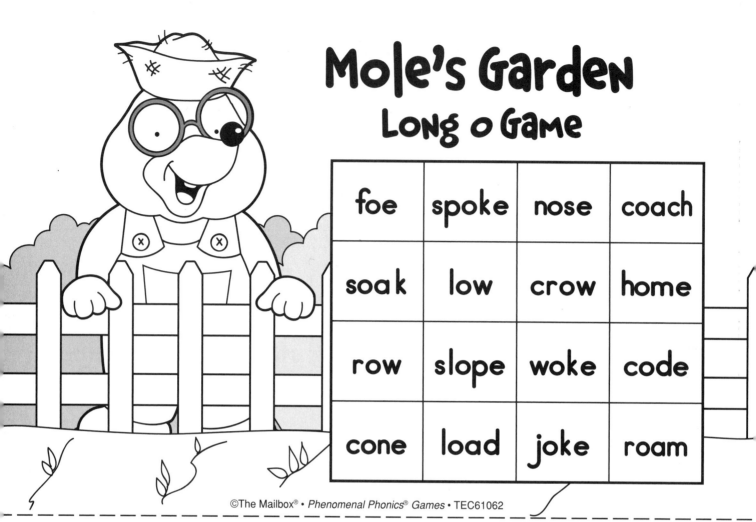

foe	spoke	nose	coach
soak	low	crow	home
row	slope	woke	code
cone	load	joke	roam

Mole's Garden
Long o Game

froze	pole	roam	toe
flow	chose	stone	hose
coal	bone	cone	loaf
poke	row	zone	grow

Mole's Garden
Long o Game

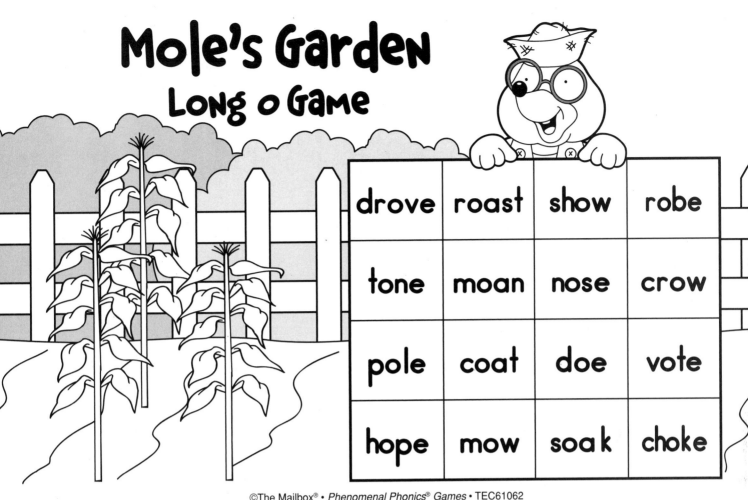

drove	roast	show	robe
tone	moan	nose	crow
pole	coat	doe	vote
hope	mow	soak	choke

Mole's Garden
Long o Game

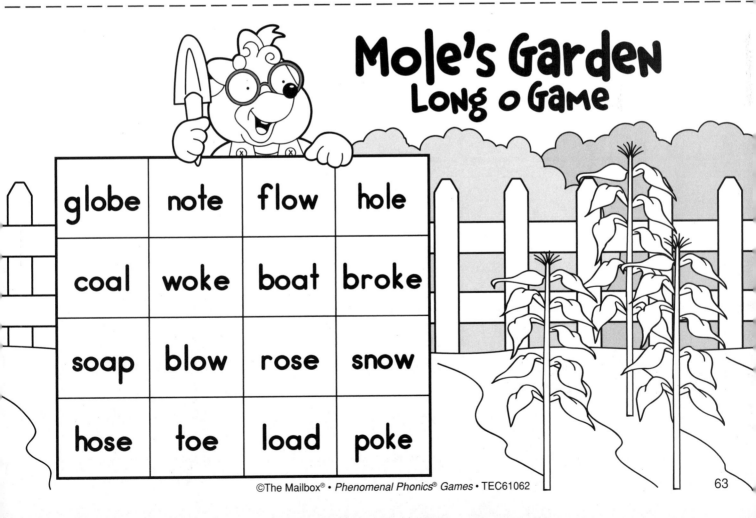

globe	note	flow	hole
coal	woke	boat	broke
soap	blow	rose	snow
hose	toe	load	poke

boat	coach	coal	coat	float
goal	goat	load	loaf	loan
moan	road	roam	roast	soak
soap	doe	foe	toe	bone
broke	choke	chose	code	cone
drove	froze	globe	hole	home

TEC61062 (on each card)

hope	hose	joke	nose	note
TEC61062	TEC61062	TEC61062	TEC61062	TEC61062
poke	pole	robe	rope	rose
TEC61062	TEC61062	TEC61062	TEC61062	TEC61062
slope	smoke	spoke	stone	those
TEC61062	TEC61062	TEC61062	TEC61062	TEC61062
tone	vote	woke	zone	blow
TEC61062	TEC61062	TEC61062	TEC61062	TEC61062
crow	flow	glow	grow	low
TEC61062	TEC61062	TEC61062	TEC61062	TEC61062
mow	row	show	slow	snow
TEC61062	TEC61062	TEC61062	TEC61062	TEC61062

Off to School

Circle the correct word for each picture.

bap
bat
ban

nat
nan
nap

fan
fap
fat

hap
hat
han

Dino Bus

✏ Write each word.

Note to the teacher: Use with the directions on page 6.

Name _____

Sunken Treasure

Circle the correct word for each picture.

brip
brin
brick

chip
chin
chick

ship
shin
shick

stin
stip
stick

 Write each word.

_____

_____

_____

_____

_____

_____

Note to the teacher: Use with the directions on page 12.

Soup's On!

Circle the correct word for each picture.

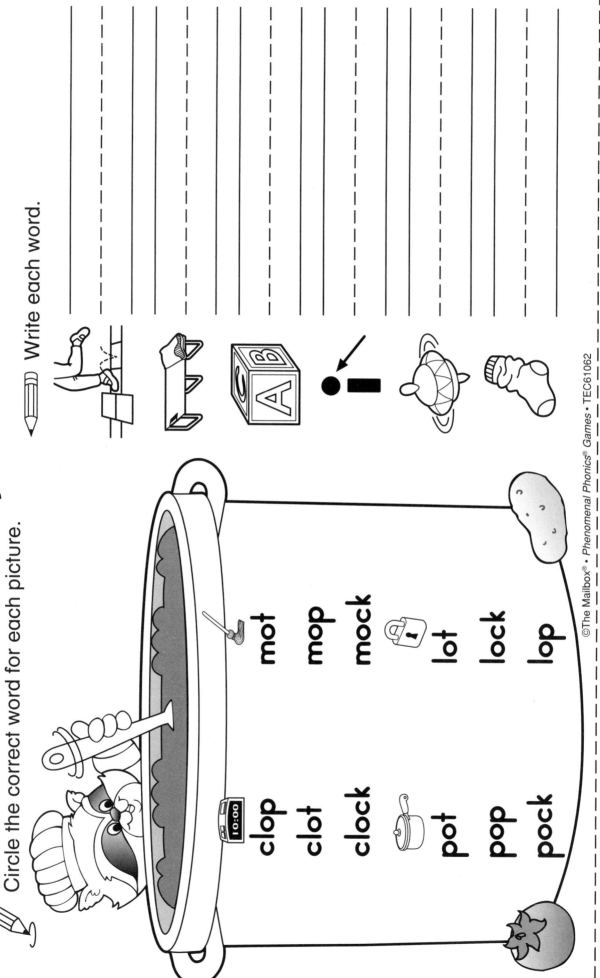

clop	mot
clot	mop
clock	mock
pot	lot
pop	lock
pock	lop

Write each word.

Note to the teacher: Use with the directions on page 18.

Yummy Honey!

 Circle the correct word for each picture.

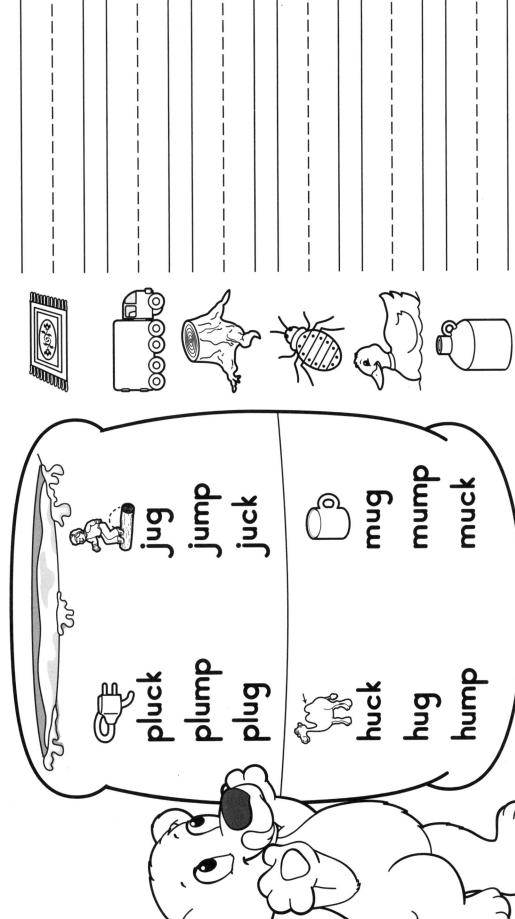

pluck
plump
plug

jug
jump
juck

huck
hug
hump

mug
mump
muck

 Write each word.

©The Mailbox® • *Phenomenal Phonics*® *Games* • TEC61062

Note to the teacher: Use with the directions on page 24.

A Word Family Celebration

Circle the correct word for each picture.

can cap	pin pick	sop sock	juck jug

Write the word.

1.  _____

2.  _____

3.  _____

4. _____

5.  _____

6.  _____

7. 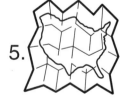 _____

8.  _____

Note to the teacher: Use after completing the games on pages 6, 12, 18, and 24.

Assessment of blends
sk, sl, sn, sp, st, sw

Special Delivery!

✏️ Circle the beginning blend for each picture.

✏️ Write the blend to complete each word.

oon _____

ide _____

ar _____

ate _____

ing _____

ake _____

	🕷️ sp	🧥 sk	🪥 sw	🛷 sk	🐌 st
	st	sl	sk	sp	sn
	sl	sw	st	sl	sp
	sk	sn	sp	sn	sw
USA 39¢	sn	sw	sl	st	

©The Mailbox® • *Phenomenal Phonics*® *Games* • TEC61062

Note to the teacher: Use with the directions on page 30.

Assessment of blends
bl, br, cl, cr, fl, fr, gl, gr

Hanging Out to Dry

Circle the beginning blend for each picture.

✏️ Write the blend to complete each word.

_____ ag

_____ ick

_____ ab

_____ og

_____ ock

_____ obe

Circle the beginning blend for each picture.

fl	br	fr	gr
bl	cr	gl	bl
br	gl	fl	fr
cr	gr	cr	cl

gl	fl	cl	cr
br	cl	gl	gr
fl	gr	fr	cl
fr	br	gr	bl

Note to the teacher: Use with the directions on page 36.

Assessment of long *a* spellings

Later, Gator!

Circle each correct spelling.

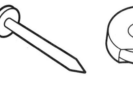

kaij
cage
kage

drane
trayne
train

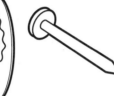

tray
tay
trae

graip
grapes
grayp

Write each word.

Note to the teacher: Use with the directions on page 42.

73

Time for Ice Cream

Circle each correct spelling.

pie
py
pigh

nyt
night
nite

fligh
flie
fly

kight
kite
kyte

Write each word.

©The Mailbox® • *Phenomenal Phonics*® *Games* • TEC61062

Note to the teacher: Use with the directions on page 48.

Eager Beaver

Circle each correct spelling.

 peche

pech

peach

 cheek

cheak

cheke

 jeyp

jeep

jepe

 beed

beyd

bead

✏️ Write each word.

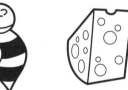

Note to the teacher: Use with the directions on page 54.

Assessment of long o spellings

Mole's Garden

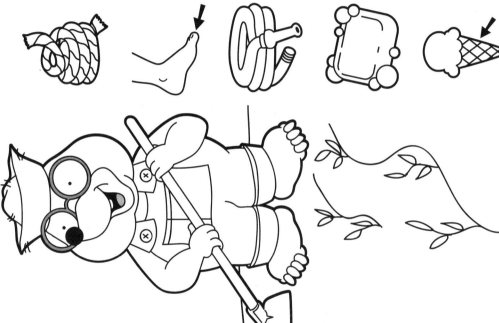

✏️ Write each word.

✏️ Circle each correct spelling.

bone
boan
boen

snoe
snow
snoa

bote
boat
bowt

glowb
gloab
globe

Note to the teacher: Use with the directions on page 60.

A Long-Vowel Celebration

Circle the correct spelling.

nale nail nayl	kyte kight kite	bee bea bey	roep rope rowp

Write the word.

1.  _____

2.  _____

3.  _____

4. 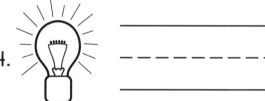 _____

5.  _____

6. 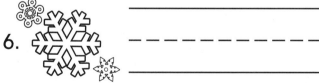 _____

7.  _____

8. 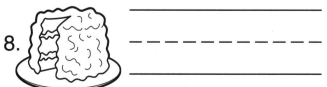 _____

Storage Labels

Copy and cut out the storage labels on pages 78–80. Glue each label to a large manila envelope. Then place copies of the corresponding student gameboards and teacher cards inside each envelope. If desired, store a copy of the teacher page, copies of the corresponding brag tags, and game markers in the envelopes as well.

Use with the games described on pages 6 and 12.

Off to School
Short a Word Families Game

TEC61062

Sunken Treasure
Short i Word Families Game

TEC61062

Yummy Honey!
Short u Word Families
Game

Hanging Out to Dry
Blends Game
bl, br, cl, cr, fl, fr, gl, gr

Soup's On!
Short o Word Families
Game

Special Delivery
Blends Game
sk, sl, sn, sp, st, sw

Storage Labels

Use with the games described on pages 42, 48, 54, and 60.

Time for Ice Cream
Long *i* Game

TEC61062

Mole's Garden
Long *o* Game

TEC61062

Later, Gator!
Long *a* Game

TEC61062

Eager Beaver
Long *e* Game

TEC61062